Blockchain Beginners:

Smart Contracts

A Simple Overview and Guide

To Smart Contracts

By Nan00t

This book is directed to beginners and blockchain enthusiasts. It provides an overview of blockchain smart contracts supplemented with insight, examples, and resources for one starting to familiarize within the Web3 landscape.

Table of Contents

Chapter 1

Introduction to Blockchain Technology

Blockchain technology is a relatively new and rapidly evolving field, with the potential to revolutionize industries from finance to healthcare to supply chain management. At its core, a blockchain is a decentralized, digital ledger that records transactions across a network of computers.

The first and most well-known application of blockchain technology is the digital currency, Bitcoin. Created in 2009 by an unknown individual or group of individuals using the pseudonym Satoshi Nakamoto, Bitcoin is the first successful implementation of a blockchain-based system. Without the need for a central authority, such as a bank or government, it allows for peer-to-peer transactions.

A key feature of blockchain technology is its decentralized nature. Unlike traditional systems, which rely on a central authority to maintain and update the ledger, a blockchain is maintained by a network of computers, or nodes, that work together to validate and record transactions. This decentralization provides several advantages, including increased security and transparency, as well as the ability to enable trust in situations where it would otherwise be difficult or impossible.

Blockchains are essentially a chain of blocks that contain information. Each block contains a set of transactions and a unique code, called a "hash," that links it to the previous block. Once a block is added to the chain, the information it contains is considered to be a permanent part of the blockchain, which cannot be changed without the network's consensus. This makes blockchains highly resistant to tampering and fraud.

There are several different types of blockchains, each with their own features and characteristics. The most common types are:

Public blockchains: These are open to anyone and are typically used for cryptocurrencies like Bitcoin or Ethereum.

Private blockchains: These are restricted to a certain group of users, such as a company or organization, and are typically used for internal systems or supply chain management.

Consortium blockchains: These are a hybrid of public and private blockchains, and are typically used for specific industries or groups of companies.

In addition to these three types, there are also sidechains, which are separate blockchains that are linked to a main blockchain, and hybrid blockchains, which combine features of both public and private blockchains. More on this in the next chapter.

To sum up, Blockchain technology is a decentralized and digital ledger technology that records transactions across a network of computers. It is the backbone of the first and most well-known application of blockchain technology, Bitcoin and also other cryptocurrencies. A secure and transparent way to store and transfer data that holds several advantages over traditional systems. There are several types of blockchains each with their own characteristics and use cases, public, private and consortium blockchains being the most common.

Chapter 2

Introduction to Smart Contracts

Smart contracts are self-executing contracts with the terms of agreement written directly into lines of code. This code created by a developer familiar with the programming language is designed to facilitate, verify, and enforce the negotiation or performance of said contract. They were first proposed by computer scientist Nick Szabo in 1994, who described them as "a set of promises, specified in digital form, including protocols within which the parties perform on these promises."

One of the key features of smart contracts is their ability to automatically execute the terms of a contract without the need for intermediaries. For example, a traditional contract for the purchase of a house might require the services of a real estate agent, a lawyer, and a title company to ensure terms of the contract are met. In contrast, a smart contract for the purchase of a house could automatically transfer ownership of the house from the seller to the buyer once all of the terms of the contract, such as the payment of the purchase price, have been met.

Smart contracts are typically created using a programming language, Solidity, which runs on Ethereum, a blockchain specifically designed to support the creation of decentralized applications (dApps) and smart contracts. Decentralized Applications (dApps) are a type of application that runs on a blockchain network. They are different from traditional applications in that they are not controlled by a single entity and are decentralized. They run on a peer-to-peer network and can be programmed to operate on multiple blockchain platforms.

Smart contracts have a wide range of potential use cases, including:

Financial Services: Smart contracts can be used to automate the process of issuing and trading financial instruments, such as stocks and bonds. They can also be used to create decentralized exchanges, where users can trade cryptocurrencies without the need for a central authority.

Supply Chain Management: Smart contracts can be used to track the movement of goods through a supply chain, from the point of origin to the point of consumption.

Healthcare: Smart contracts can be used to securely store and share medical records, as well as to automate the process of claims management and payment.

Voting: Smart contracts can be used to create decentralized voting systems that are transparent and difficult to manipulate.

Real Estate: Smart contracts can be used to automate the process of buying and selling property, including the transfer of ownership and the payment of taxes and fees.

Gaming: Smart contracts can be used to create decentralized, blockchain-based games where players can earn and trade in-game assets.

They have the potential to greatly improve the efficiency and security of many industries and processes. However, they are not without their challenges. One of the main challenges facing the implementation of smart contracts is scalability. The current infrastructure of most blockchain networks is not able to handle the high volume of transactions that would be required for widespread adoption of smart contracts. Additionally, smart contracts are vulnerable to bugs and errors in the code, which could lead to unintended consequences.

The lack of legal recognition for smart contracts is another challenge. In most jurisdictions, smart contracts are not yet recognized as legally binding. This means that in the event of a dispute, it may be difficult to enforce the terms of a smart contract.

There are several ways to address the scalability and legal recognition issues in smart contract projects:

To address the issue of legal recognition, one may work with legal experts and regulators to educate and learn about the benefits and potential use cases of smart contracts from both sides. This can help to build support for the recognition and regulation of smart contracts in different jurisdictions.

Another approach is to design smart contracts that are compliant with existing laws and regulations. This can help to increase the chances of them being recognized and enforced by the legal system.

One approach to addressing scalability issues is to use off-chain scaling solutions, such as state channels and sidechains. These solutions allow for some or all of the computations and transactions in a smart contract to be conducted off the blockchain, reducing the load on the main chain, thereby increasing the number of transactions that can be processed.

Another approach is the use of sharding, which is a method of dividing a blockchain network into smaller, more manageable pieces, or "shards." This allows each shard to process transactions in parallel, increasing the overall throughput of the network.

It's worth noting that Blockchain technology and smart contracts are relatively new and evolving fields, so it's important to stay up to date with the latest developments and best practices in order to improve and evolve.

Let's dive deeper into the different featured smart contracts!

Interoperable Smart Contracts

Interoperable smart contracts are smart contracts that are designed to work across different blockchain networks and enable different blockchain systems to communicate with one another. They are a type of multi-chain smart contract, which can run on multiple blockchain networks simultaneously and are designed to enable the transfer of assets, data, and value between different blockchain networks.

One of the main values of interoperable smart contracts is that they enable the creation of decentralized applications and businesses that can operate across different blockchain networks. This allows for the creation of more complex and sophisticated decentralized applications that can take advantage of

the unique features and capabilities of
different blockchain networks.

Another value of interoperable
smart contracts is that they can
increase the scalability of
decentralized applications by allowing
them to run on multiple blockchain
networks simultaneously. This can
handle a larger volume of transactions
and data than a single blockchain
network would be able to handle.

Additionally, interoperable smart
contracts can provide more security and
immutability for decentralized
applications by running on multiple
blockchain networks. This can reduce
the risk of attacks or failures on a
single network and increase the
resilience of the overall system.

Interoperable smart contracts also
can help to overcome the issue of
fragmentation in the blockchain
ecosystem. With interoperable smart
contracts, different blockchain
networks can communicate with one
another, leading to a more connected
and cohesive ecosystem where different

blockchain networks can work together
and build on one another's strengths.

Cross-chain compatibility:
Interoperable smart contracts are
designed to be compatible with multiple
blockchain networks, allowing them to
run on different blockchain systems and
interact with them. This allows for the
creation of decentralized applications
and businesses that can operate across
different blockchain networks.

Scalability: Interoperable smart
contracts can increase the scalability
of decentralized applications by
allowing them to run on multiple
blockchain networks simultaneously.
This can handle a larger volume of
transactions and data than a single
blockchain network would be able to
handle.

Security: Interoperable smart contracts
can provide more security and
immutability for decentralized
applications by running on multiple

blockchain networks. This can reduce the risk of attacks or failures on a single network and increase the resilience of the overall system.

Flexibility: Interoperable smart contracts allow for greater flexibility in choosing the best blockchain network for a specific use case based on factors such as transaction speed, fees, security, and compliance requirements.

Overcoming fragmentation: Interoperable smart contracts can help overcome the issue of fragmentation in the blockchain ecosystem by allowing different blockchain networks to communicate with one another and work together.

In summary, interoperable smart contracts offer a range of benefits, including increased interoperability, scalability, security, and flexibility. These benefits are expected to drive the adoption of interoperable smart

contracts in various industries, and
will lead to the creation of new
decentralized applications and business
models that can take advantage of the
unique features of different blockchain
networks.

Hybrid Smart Contracts

These are a combination of
off-chain and on-chain smart contracts.
They use off-chain data and
computations to achieve better
scalability and privacy and then use
on-chain smart contracts to ensure
security and immutability.

Off-chain refers to transactions
or data that are conducted outside of
the blockchain, while on-chain refers
to transactions or data that are
recorded and stored on the blockchain.

Off-chain transactions are not
recorded on the blockchain and do not
require the use of the network's native
cryptocurrency. They are typically
faster and cheaper than on-chain
transactions because they don't require

the same level of security and validation.

On-chain transactions, on the other hand, are recorded on the blockchain and require the use of the network's native cryptocurrency. These transactions are typically slower and more expensive than off-chain transactions, but they offer a higher level of security and immutability.

In short, on-chain transactions are recorded on the blockchain and therefore, transparent and permanent, while off-chain transactions are not recorded on the blockchain and are not transparent and permanent.

A hybrid smart contract is a type of smart contract that combines features of both on-chain and off-chain smart contracts. It is a combination of the two where some part of the contract is executed on the blockchain while some parts are executed off-chain.

One of the main values of hybrid smart contracts is that they can increase the scalability of decentralized applications by offloading some of the computations and data storage to off-chain systems. This can reduce the load on the blockchain network and make it more efficient.

Another value of hybrid smart contracts is that they can provide more privacy for decentralized applications by allowing for off-chain execution of sensitive or private data. This can protect the privacy of users and make it more difficult for adversaries to access or tamper with sensitive data.

They can also provide more flexibility in choosing the best execution environment for a specific use case based on factors such as transaction speed, fees, security, and privacy requirements.

Hybrid smart contracts are unique from other smart contract models in that they combine the benefits of both on-chain and off-chain execution. On-chain smart contracts provide security, immutability and transparency, while off-chain smart contracts provide scalability and privacy. Hybrid smart contracts allow for a balance between the two, allowing for the use of the best features of both types of smart contracts depending on the use case.

In summary, hybrid smart contracts offer a range of benefits, including increased scalability, privacy, and flexibility. These benefits are expected to drive the adoption of hybrid smart contracts in various industries, and will lead to the creation of new decentralized applications and business models that can take advantage of the unique features of both on-chain and off-chain smart contracts.

State Channel Smart Contracts

These are used to create off-chain smart contracts that can be executed without the need for the entire network to validate each transaction. They can be used to increase the scalability and speed of smart contract execution, while still maintaining the security and immutability of on-chain smart contracts.

An example could be the Lightning Network, a second-layer solution built on top of the Bitcoin blockchain that enables fast, low-cost transactions. It uses state channels to open a direct payment channel between two parties, enabling them to transact without the need for each transaction to be recorded on the blockchain. This allows for faster, cheaper and more private transactions while still leveraging the security of the underlying blockchain. Other examples of state channel smart contracts include Raiden Network for Ethereum and the Perun Network for Bitcoin Cash.

dApp-chain Smart Contracts

These are smart contracts that are specific to a particular decentralized application (DApp) and can be used to create custom functionality and rules for that DApp. They can be used to create more advanced and customized decentralized applications.

A DApp-chain (Decentralized application-specific chain) smart contract is a type of smart contract that runs on a blockchain network specifically designed for a specific decentralized application or use case. Dapp-chain smart contracts are unique from other smart contract models in that they are designed to optimize the performance and security of a specific decentralized application, rather than being a general-purpose smart contract that can be used for any application.

One of the main values of Dapp-chain smart contracts is that they can increase the performance and efficiency of a specific decentralized application. By designing a blockchain network specifically for a specific use case, Dapp-chain smart contracts can optimize the network's consensus mechanism, data storage, and other features to meet the specific requirements of the application.

Another value of Dapp-chain smart contracts is that they can provide more security for a specific decentralized application. By creating a dedicated blockchain network for a specific use case, Dapp-chain smart contracts can reduce the risk of attacks or failures on the network and increase the resilience of the overall system.

Dapp-chain smart contracts can also provide more flexibility in choosing the best blockchain network for a specific use case based on factors such as transaction speed, fees, security, and compliance requirements.

Some popular examples of dApps built on Ethereum include CryptoKitties, a blockchain-based virtual game where players can buy, sell, and breed virtual cats, and Uniswap, a decentralized exchange for trading cryptocurrency. These dApps are built using smart contracts that run on

the Ethereum blockchain, and they are
considered DApp-chain smart contracts.

In summary, Dapp-chain smart
contracts are designed to optimize the
performance and security of a specific
decentralized application. They can
increase the performance and efficiency
of a specific decentralized
application, provide more security, and
provide more flexibility in choosing
the best blockchain network for a
specific use case. This allows for the
creation of new decentralized
applications and business models that
can take advantage of the unique
features of Dapp-chain smart contracts.

Sidechain Smart Contracts

These are smart contracts that are
connected to a main blockchain network,
but operate on a separate sidechain.
They can be used to increase the
scalability and speed of smart contract
execution, while still maintaining the

security and immutability of the main blockchain network.

A sidechain smart contract is a type of smart contract that runs on a separate blockchain network, called a sidechain, that is connected to a parent blockchain network, called the mainchain. The mainchain and sidechain are connected through a mechanism called a two-way peg, which allows for the transfer of assets and information between the two chains.

One of the main values of sidechain smart contracts is that they can increase the scalability and performance of decentralized applications by offloading some of the computations and data storage to the sidechain. This can reduce the load on the mainchain network and make it more efficient.

Another value of sidechain smart contracts is that they can provide more flexibility in choosing the best blockchain network for a specific use case based on factors such as transaction speed, fees, security, and privacy requirements. By allowing for the creation of specialized sidechains for specific use cases, sidechain smart contracts can provide a more optimized environment for those use cases, while still allowing for the benefits of the mainchain network.

A popular example of a sidechain smart contract is the Plasma project, developed by Ethereum co-founder Vitalik Buterin and Joseph Poon. Plasma is a framework for building decentralized applications on top of the Ethereum blockchain. It allows for the creation of child chains, called Plasma chains, that run parallel to the main Ethereum chain. These child chains can handle their own transactions and smart contracts, and can also interact with the main chain to access the security provided by the larger network. This allows for increased scalability, as transactions can be processed on the side chains rather than clogging the main chain. More on this scaling technique in Chapter 6.

In summary, sidechain smart
contracts offer a range of benefits,
including increased scalability,
flexibility, and security. These
benefits are expected to drive the
adoption of sidechain smart contracts
in various industries, and will lead to
the creation of new decentralized
applications and business models that
can take advantage of the unique
features of sidechain smart contracts.

These are smart contracts that
allow for the creation of cross-chain
applications that can run multiple
blockchain networks simultaneously.
They can take advantage of the unique
features and capabilities of different
blockchain platforms, such as high
throughput, low fees, security, and
immutability for example. That said,
one of the main values of multi-chain
smart contracts is the possibilities of
interoperability between different
blockchain networks. This means that
different blockchain systems can
communicate with one another, allowing

for the transfer of assets, data, and value between them. This opens up new possibilities for decentralized applications and businesses that can operate across multiple blockchain networks.

Another value of multi-chain smart contracts is increasing the scalability of decentralized applications. By running on multiple blockchain networks, these smart contracts can handle a larger volume of transactions and data than a single blockchain network would be able to handle.

Additionally, multi-chain smart contracts can provide more security and immutability for decentralized applications. By running on multiple blockchain networks, these smart contracts can be less vulnerable to attacks or failures on a single network.

They also provide more flexibility for businesses and developers, by choosing the best blockchain network for their specific use case based on factors such as transaction speed,

fees, security, and compliance
requirements.

One example of a multi-chain smart
contract would be Manifold. Manifold
smart contracts are a type of smart
contract that are designed to run on
multiple blockchain networks
simultaneously. This allows for the
creation of cross-chain applications
and the ability to leverage the unique
features and capabilities of different
blockchain platforms.

Manifold smart contracts are
typically implemented using a technique
called "atomic swaps." Atomic swaps
allow for the exchange of one
cryptocurrency for another without the
need for a centralized intermediary.
This is accomplished by creating a
smart contract that holds both of the
currencies and automatically releases
one of them to the other party once
certain conditions are met.

One of the main benefits of
Manifold smart contracts is the ability
to take advantage of the different

features and capabilities of different
blockchain networks. For example, a
Manifold smart contract could use the
high throughput and low fees of one
blockchain for high-frequency
transactions, while using the security
and immutability of another blockchain
for long-term storage of sensitive
data.

Another benefit of Manifold smart
contracts is the ability to create
cross-chain decentralized applications
(dApps).

It's worth noting that Manifold
smart contracts are relatively new and
still evolving. There are still some
challenges that need to be addressed,
such as the lack of standardization and
interoperability across different
blockchain networks. Some blockchain
networks may not support the execution
of smart contracts, making it difficult
to create Manifold smart contracts on
these networks.

Multi-chain smart contracts offer
a range of benefits, including

increased interoperability, scalability, security, and flexibility. These benefits are expected to drive the adoption of multi-chain smart contracts in various industries, and will lead to the creation of new decentralized applications and business models that can take advantage of the unique features of different blockchain networks.

These are a few examples of different types of smart contracts that allow for the creation of cross-chain applications, interoperability, scalability, and security. It's worth noting that these types of smart contracts are relatively new and still evolving, so the possibilities are vast and new types of smart contracts may emerge in the future.

Chapter 3

Understanding Ethereum and its Popular
Use Cases of Smart Contracts

Ethereum is an open-source,
decentralized platform that enables the
creation and deployment of smart
contracts. It is built on the
blockchain technology and provides
developers with a powerful toolset for
creating decentralized applications
(dApps).

Ethereum uses its own programming
language, called Solidity, which is
similar to JavaScript and is used to
write smart contracts. These contracts
are self-executing and can be
programmed to automatically execute
certain actions when certain conditions
are met.

One of the key features of
Ethereum is its use of Ether (ETH) as
its native cryptocurrency. Ether is
used to pay for the computational

resources required to execute smart
contracts and is also used as a means
of exchange within the Ethereum
ecosystem.

Ethereum also provides a
decentralized virtual machine (EVM)
that executes smart contracts. The EVM
is a global, public computer that can
be used by anyone, and it ensures that
all smart contracts are executed in the
same way, regardless of the user or
device that initiates the contract.

One of the most popular use cases
for Ethereum smart contracts is the
creation of decentralized exchanges
(DEXs). DEXs are online platforms that
allow users to buy and sell
cryptocurrencies without the need for a
central authority or intermediary.
Instead, transactions are executed
automatically by smart contracts and
are recorded on the Ethereum
blockchain.

Another popular use case for
Ethereum smart contracts is the
creation of decentralized autonomous

organizations (DAOs). DAOs are decentralized organizations that run by a set of rules encoded in their smart contracts. These rules determine how the organization is governed, how funds are raised and spent, and how decisions are made. More on these in Chapter 6!

Ethereum smart contracts can also be used to create non-fungible tokens (NFTs), which are unique digital assets that can be bought, sold, and traded like traditional assets. NFTs are commonly used in the gaming and collectibles industries, and they allow for the creation of digital assets that are truly one-of-a-kind.

It's worth noting that Ethereum is not the only platform for smart contracts, there are other blockchain platforms such as EOS, TRON, and others that also support smart contract functionality. However, Ethereum is currently the most widely used and widely supported platform for smart contracts.

To develop on the Ethereum network, developers need to use a specific set of tools and frameworks like web3.js, Truffle, and OpenZeppelin. These tools provide developers with the necessary libraries and frameworks for interacting with the Ethereum blockchain and deploying smart contracts.

In summary, Ethereum is a powerful and versatile platform for the creation and deployment of smart contracts. Its decentralized nature, use of Ether, and powerful toolset make it an attractive option for developers and businesses looking to build decentralized applications and automate complex processes.

Chapter 4

Developing and Deploying Smart
Contracts

As we discussed in the previous
chapters, smart contracts are
self-executing contracts with the terms
of the agreement between buyer and
seller being directly written into
lines of code. This chapter will guide
you through the process of developing
and deploying your own smart contracts.

The first step in developing a
smart contract is to choose a
development platform. There are several
platforms available such as Ethereum,
EOS, TRON, and more. Each platform has
its own set of programming languages
and development tools. Ethereum, for
example, uses Solidity as its
programming language, while EOS uses
C++. Choose a platform that is best
suited for your project and that you
are comfortable working with, but if

you are new to programming language it's best advised to consult and hire a developer specialized and experienced in creating and customizing smart contracts. More on this later...

Ethereum is the most popular platform for developing smart contracts and decentralized applications (dApps). It has a large developer community and a wide range of tools and resources available for building and deploying smart contracts. It also supports a programming language called Solidity, which is specifically designed for writing smart contracts.

EOS is a high-performance blockchain platform that is designed for building decentralized applications with a high degree of scalability. It has a unique consensus algorithm called Delegated Proof of Stake (DPoS) which allows for faster transaction speeds and greater scalability compared to other platforms.

TRON is a blockchain platform that is focused on the entertainment industry, and it is designed to support high-throughput and low-latency use cases. It also supports Solidity and is focused on building decentralized applications that can handle large amounts of data and traffic.

Hyperledger is an open-source project that provides a set of tools and frameworks for building private and permissioned blockchain networks. It supports multiple programming languages like Go, Java, JavaScript, and more. It is mainly used for enterprise solutions and consortium networks.

Corda is a blockchain platform that is designed for financial services use cases. It is focused on privacy and security, and it allows for the creation of smart contracts that can be executed only by the parties involved in the contract.

R3 Corda is a blockchain platform built on Corda, it is designed for enterprise solutions and consortium networks, it allows for the integration of smart contracts and dApps with legacy systems and provides a high degree of scalability and security.

Some other notable mentions with unique capabilities:

NEM is a blockchain platform that is designed for enterprise use cases, such as supply chain management, digital identity, and asset tracking. It has a unique consensus algorithm called Proof of Importance (PoI) which takes into account a user's overall importance to the network.

Lisk is a blockchain platform that is designed for building decentralized applications with a focus on modularity. It allows developers to build and deploy their own sidechains, which can be customized to suit the specific requirements of the project.

Aion is a blockchain platform that is designed for interoperability between different blockchain networks. It allows for the creation of multi-tier architectures that can connect different blockchain networks and enable the transfer of data and value between them.

IOTA is a blockchain platform that is focused on the Internet of Things (IoT) use cases. It uses a unique consensus algorithm called the Tangle, which allows for fast and fee-less transactions.

Hashgraph is a distributed ledger technology that is designed to be faster and more secure than traditional blockchain technology. It uses a unique consensus algorithm called the Gossip protocol, which allows for high-throughput and low-latency use cases. A high-throughput and low-latency use case for blockchain and smart contracts would be a financial application, such as a high-frequency trading platform or a payment processing system. These types of applications require quick processing times and the ability to handle a large number of transactions simultaneously. Blockchain technology, with its ability to process multiple transactions simultaneously through the use of parallel processing, can provide the necessary throughput. Additionally, smart contracts can be used to automate the execution of trades or payments, further reducing latency. Another example of high-throughput and low-latency use cases is supply chain management where a smart contract can automate the process of supply chain management, making it more efficient and less time consuming.

Solana is a blockchain platform that is designed for high-throughput use cases, it allows for the scaling of decentralized applications and its transaction speed can handle up to 65,000 transactions per second.

These platforms may be less well-known than some of the more established blockchain platforms like Ethereum, but they still have unique capabilities that may make them suitable for certain types of projects. As always, the choice of platform will depend on the specific requirements of the project, which can be determined when working closely with a developer or becoming specialized in the area.

Once you have chosen a development platform, the next step is writing the programming language used to write that contract or working with a developer! The most popular programming languages for writing smart contracts are Solidity (Ethereum), C++ (EOS), and Solidity (TRON).

If you are not programmer, here are some resources one can find someone specialized in the programming language for smart contracts:

Upwork: Upwork is a platform that connects businesses and freelancers from all over the world. You can find and hire smart contract developers with experience in various blockchain platforms like Ethereum, EOS, TRON, and more.

Freelancer: Freelancer is another platform that connects businesses and freelancers. You can find and hire smart contract developers with experience in various blockchain platforms like Ethereum, EOS, TRON, and more.

Blocklancer: Blocklancer is a freelance platform that operates on the Ethereum blockchain. This platform is specifically designed for blockchain and smart contract development projects, and you can find and hire smart contract developers with experience in various blockchain platforms like Ethereum, EOS, TRON, and more.

Gitcoin: Gitcoin is a platform for open-source development that runs on the Ethereum blockchain. You can find and hire smart contract developers with experience in various blockchain platforms like Ethereum, EOS, TRON, and more.

Toptal: Toptal is a platform that specializes in connecting businesses with top freelance talent. You can find and hire smart contract developers with experience in various blockchain platforms like Ethereum, EOS, TRON, and more.

Blockchain Developer: Blockchain Developer is a platform that connects businesses and developers who have experience in blockchain and smart contract development. One can find and hire smart contract developers with experience in various blockchain platforms like Ethereum, EOS, TRON, and more.

And of course reaching out to one's Web3 network is a great way as well.

When hiring a smart contract developer, it's important to check their experience and portfolio of work, as well as their availability and communication skills. It's also a good idea to have a clear understanding of your project requirements and expectations before working with them. They will be writing, testing, and deploying the contract, and potentially tending to any bug fixes in the future. It's important to keep in mind that smart contracts are immutable and cannot be altered once they are deployed, so it's crucial to thoroughly test your code before deployment to ensure that it will function as intended. This can be done using a test network or a virtual machine.

Once your contract is deployed, it will be stored on the blockchain and can be interacted with by other users. To interact with the contract, you will

need to use a wallet or other software
that allows you to call the functions
of the contract. This is known as
"invoking" the contract. The contract
will then execute the code and perform
the specified action.

Interacting with a smart contract
is the process of sending transactions
to the contract on the blockchain to
execute its defined functions or
methods. The purpose of interacting
with a contract is to initiate actions
on the blockchain, such as transferring
assets, updating data stored on the
blockchain, or triggering other smart
contract functions. This is an
important step in the process of using
a smart contract as it allows users to
utilize the capabilities and features
of the contract. Some common ways of
interacting with a smart contract
include using a wallet or browser
extension, connecting to a web3 API, or
using a command line interface. The
specific method will depend on the

platform and programming language used
to develop the contract.

After deploying your contract, it
is important to monitor it to ensure
that it is functioning as intended. If
there are any bugs or errors, you will
need to update the contract. Updating a
contract is similar to deploying a new
contract, but it requires a slightly
different process.

Monitoring a smart contract
involves tracking the activity and
performance of the contract on the
blockchain. This can include monitoring
the execution of transactions, the
storage of data on the blockchain, and
any changes to the contract's code or
state. Some common tools used for
monitoring smart contracts include
blockchain explorers, event logs, and
monitoring dashboards.

Blockchain explorers are web-based
applications that allow you to view the
entire history of a smart contract,
including all the transactions and
internal state changes. They provide a
user-friendly interface to view the

details of the contract, including the code, the transactions, and the internal state.

Some popular blockchain explorers include:

Etherscan: This explorer is specific to the Ethereum blockchain and allows users to view transactions, addresses, and contract information.

Blockchair: This explorer provides information on multiple blockchain networks including Bitcoin, Ethereum, Bitcoin Cash, and Litecoin.

Blockscout: It is an open-source explorer that supports Ethereum and Ethereum Classic.

BTC.com: This explorer is specific to the Bitcoin blockchain and allows users to view transactions, addresses, and block information.

Blockchain.com: It is a popular explorer that supports Bitcoin and Bitcoin Cash.

Blockstream: It is another popular blockchain explorer which is user-friendly and provides a lot of information about the bitcoin blockchain.

CoinGecko: It is a cryptocurrency data platform that also provides blockchain explorer features for multiple blockchain networks.

CryptoID: it is a blockchain explorer that supports multiple blockchain networks like Bitcoin, Litecoin, and Dogecoin.

These are just a few examples, and there are many more blockchain explorers available for different blockchain networks.

Event logs are a way to track specific events that occur within a

smart contract. These events can
include things like token transfers,
data updates, or other actions that
happen within the contract. Event logs
can be accessed and monitored through
the use of web3 libraries or other
tools that are compatible with the
specific blockchain platform.

Some web3 libraries:

Ethereum's event logs can be accessed
using tools like Truffle and web3.js

EOSIO's action traces can be accessed
using tools like cleos and eosjs

Hyperledger's transaction event logs
can be accessed using the Hyperledger
Explorer or custom-built tools using
the Hyperledger Fabric SDK.

Bitcoin's transaction logs can be
accessed using tools like Bitcoin Core
or blockchain explorers such as
blockchain.com or blockstream.info

Monitoring dashboards are web-based tools that provide a visual representation of the activity and performance of a smart contract. They can display information such as the number of transactions, the amount of gas used, and the current state of the contract. Dashboards can also include alerts and notifications to notify users of any issues or changes in the contract.

Some popular monitoring dashboards:

Etherscan: A blockchain explorer for the Ethereum network that allows users to view, monitor and interact with smart contracts.

Blockchain.com: A dashboard for monitoring various aspects of the Bitcoin network, including transaction history, block details and network statistics.

DappRadar: A platform for tracking and analyzing decentralized applications (dApps) built on various blockchain networks, including Ethereum and EOS.

Blockchair: A blockchain explorer and analytics platform for multiple blockchain networks, including Bitcoin, Ethereum, and Litecoin.

CoinTracking: A platform that tracks and analyzes cryptocurrency portfolio and transaction history, allowing users to view their assets and trading activities in real-time.

Chainstack: A platform that provides tools for monitoring and managing smart contracts, as well as nodes and other infrastructure on various blockchain networks.

Infura: A service that provides API access to Ethereum and IPFS networks, allowing developers to access blockchain data without running a full node.

BlockScout: A open-source, full-featured blockchain explorer for Ethereum and EVM-based networks, which enables users to view, search, and confirm transactions and smart contract interactions.

Glassnode: A platform that offers a wide range of on-chain and network data analytics for multiple blockchain networks, including Bitcoin, Ethereum, and Litecoin.

BlockExplorer: A simple and user-friendly blockchain explorer for multiple blockchain networks, including Bitcoin, Litecoin, and Dogecoin, that allows users to view transaction history, block details and network statistics.

It's important to note that monitoring smart contracts is essential for ensuring the security and reliability of the contract, as it allows you to identify and resolve any issues or bugs that may arise. By monitoring the activity and performance of a smart contract, you can detect any potential security vulnerabilities or malicious actions that may be taking place on the contract. This can help you take action to prevent or mitigate any potential losses or damage. Monitoring can help you detect and diagnose any issues or bugs that may be affecting the contract's performance. This can help you take action to improve the reliability and functionality of the contract. Some smart contracts may need to comply with certain regulations or standards.

Monitoring can help you ensure that the contract is operating in compliance with these regulations and standards. It can also be used as part of an auditing process to ensure that the contract is operating as intended and that any transactions or changes made to the contract are valid. By understanding how the contract is being used one can identify areas where performance can be improved. This can help you make changes to the contract

that will improve its overall
efficiency and scalability.

Overall, monitoring smart
contracts is an essential aspect of
maintaining their security,
reliability, and overall performance.
It allows you to identify and resolve
issues quickly, ensuring that the
contract is operating as intended and
that any transactions or changes made
to the contract are valid.

In summary, developing and
deploying smart contracts involves
several steps such as choosing a
development platform, writing the code,
deploying the contract, interacting
with it and monitoring it. Each step
has its own set of tools and
requirements, but with the right
guidance and practice, anyone can
develop and deploy their own smart
contracts. As blockchain technology and
smart contracts are still in infancy,
there are many opportunities for
innovation and new use cases are being

discovered every day. So, this is an
exciting time to learn and start
experimenting with the technology.

Chapter 5

Smart Contract Security

As mentioned in the previous
chapter on deploying and maintaining a
smart contract, smart contract security
is a crucial aspect of blockchain
technology. It is essential for
successful deployment and execution of
the contract on a blockchain network.
Smart contracts are self-executing
digital contracts that are stored on
the blockchain and are automatically
executed when specific conditions are
met -yes! However, the decentralized
and immutable nature of blockchain
technology also makes smart contracts
vulnerable to attacks and security
breaches. Therefore, it is crucial to
consider security measures when
designing and deploying to ensure the
integrity and confidentiality of the
data stored on the blockchain.

One of the primary security
concerns with smart contracts is the
potential for malicious actors to

exploit vulnerabilities in the code.
These vulnerabilities can include
errors in the contract's logic, poor
coding practices, and lack of testing.
To mitigate these risks, it is
essential to conduct thorough testing
and code review of the smart contract
before deployment as explained in the
previous chapter. This includes testing
for potential vulnerabilities, such as
reentrancy attacks, and ensuring that
the contract's logic is sound.
Additionally, smart contract developers
should follow best practices for
coding, such as using verified
libraries and avoiding known security
pitfalls.

Another security concern with
smart contracts is the potential for
unauthorized access to the contract's
data and functionality. This can occur
through attacks such as phishing and
social engineering, where a malicious
actor tricks users into sharing their
private keys or other sensitive
information. To prevent these attacks,
it is essential to implement robust

user authentication and authorization
mechanisms in the contract, such as
multi-factor authentication and
role-based access controls.
Additionally, it is important to
educate users on the potential risks
and how to protect themselves, such as
using a hardware wallet to store their
private keys.

Smart contract security also
includes protecting against attacks on
the blockchain network itself. These
attacks can include 51% attacks, where
a malicious actor controls a majority
of the network's computing power, and
denial of service (DoS) attacks, where
the network's resources are
overwhelmed. To prevent these attacks,
it is essential to use a decentralized
blockchain network with a large and
decentralized community of users and to
implement robust consensus mechanisms.
An example of a robust consensus
mechanism is the Byzantine Fault
Tolerance (BFT) algorithm, which is
used in many blockchain platforms such
as Hyperledger, EOS, and NEO. BFT is

able to tolerate up to one-third of malicious or faulty nodes in the network and still reach consensus, making it highly resilient to attacks and failures. This makes it suitable for enterprise-grade applications where security and reliability are of paramount importance. Another example is the Delegated Proof of Stake (DPoS) which is a more energy efficient consensus mechanism that is used in platforms like EOS and TRON, it allows users to vote for delegates who in turn validate transactions and provide consensus on the network. It is considered a more efficient form of consensus mechanism. Additionally, it is important to monitor the network for any suspicious activity and to have a plan in place for responding to potential attacks.

Finally, smart contract security also includes ensuring the privacy and confidentiality of the data stored on the blockchain. This can be achieved through the use of privacy-enhancing technologies, such as zero-knowledge proofs, and by implementing robust data encryption and access controls. Additionally, it is important to comply with relevant data privacy regulations, such as the General Data Protection Regulation (GDPR) in the European Union.

In conclusion, smart contract security is a critical aspect of blockchain technology that must be considered when designing and deploying smart contracts on a blockchain network. It includes protection against code vulnerabilities, unauthorized access, network attacks, and data privacy. By following best practices for smart contract development and implementing robust security measures, it is possible to ensure the integrity and confidentiality of the data stored on the blockchain.

Chapter 6

Advanced Topics

Decentralized Finance (DeFi)

Decentralized finance, or DeFi for short, is a rapidly growing field that uses blockchain technology to create new financial applications and services that are decentralized and open to everyone. DeFi applications include lending and borrowing platforms, stablecoins, decentralized exchanges, and more. These applications have the potential to disrupt traditional financial services and provide greater access to financial services for people around the world.

Tokenization

Representing real-world assets on a blockchain is the process of tokenization. This can include anything from stocks and bonds to real estate and art. Tokenization can bring many benefits, including fractional ownership, 24/7 trading, and increased liquidity. Additionally, tokenization can also enable new forms of fundraising, such as initial coin offerings (ICOs) and security token offerings (STOs).

Token creation and management refers to the process of creating and maintaining a digital token on a blockchain network. These tokens can represent a wide variety of assets, such as cryptocurrencies, digital assets, or even physical assets. Token creation and management is important because it allows for the creation and distribution of digital assets that can be easily traded and transferred on a blockchain network. Tokens can also be used to incentivize users, create revenue streams, and provide access to certain services or products.

Oracles

Oracles are a crucial component in many blockchain-based systems as they allow smart contracts to interact with external data sources. Oracles can be used to pull data from the internet, such as stock prices or weather data, and bring that information onto the blockchain. Oracles can also be used to bring off-chain transactions onto the blockchain, such as the completion of a payment or the delivery of a physical good.

One well known oracle is Chainlink. Chainlink is a decentralized oracle network that provides secure and reliable data to smart contracts on blockchain platforms. An oracle serves as a bridge between the blockchain network and the real-world data or events, which smart contracts cannot access directly. Chainlink allows smart contracts to interact with data from various off-chain sources such as APIs, payment systems, and other blockchains, by providing them with the necessary information from a trusted source. This enables the creation of more sophisticated decentralized applications and expands the use cases

for blockchain technology. Chainlink's
decentralized architecture and use of
secure nodes provide a high level of
security and transparency, and its
open-source technology makes it
accessible to developers and businesses
of all sizes.

State Channels

As previously explained, state
channels are a way to scale blockchain
transactions by moving them off-chain.
This is done by creating a direct
channel between two parties and
conducting transactions within that
channel without the need for each
transaction to be recorded on the
blockchain. This can greatly increase
the speed and scalability of
transactions, making it possible to
conduct many more transactions per
second. With the increasing demand for
dApps that can handle high-volume
transactions with low latency, it's
likely that we will continue to see
advancements and innovations in the
area of state channel type smart

contracts, and the development of new
solutions that help to make these types
of applications even more efficient and
effective.

Sharding

Sharding as previously mentioned
is a technique for increasing the
scalability of blockchain networks. In
a sharded system, the network is
divided into smaller partitions called
shards, each of which can process
transactions independently. This can
greatly increase the number of
transactions that can be processed per
second, making it possible to scale
blockchain networks to support millions
or even billions of users. As a result,
sharded blockchain networks can handle
a much higher volume of transactions,
making them better suited for
applications that require fast and
efficient processing, such as
decentralized applications (dApps) with
large user bases. This is why we can
expect great advancements in the area
of sharding in smart contracts in the

future, as more and more people adopt blockchain technology and demand more scalable solutions.

Plasma

As explained in Chapter 2, Plasma is a technique for scaling blockchain networks that is similar to sharding. However, instead of dividing the network into smaller partitions, Plasma creates a series of "child" chains that run in parallel to the main blockchain. These child chains can handle their own transactions and then periodically "commit" their state to the main blockchain. This can greatly increase the number of transactions that can be processed per second, making it possible to scale blockchain networks to support millions or even billions of users. This is especially important for dApps that require high transaction volume or real-time data processing.

As the demand for decentralized applications continues to grow, we can expect to see further advancements in the area of plasma in order to meet

these needs and provide a more seamless
user experience.

Decentralized Apps

As previously explained DApps, or
Decentralized Applications, are a type
of software program that runs on a
blockchain network. They are unique
because they operate on a peer-to-peer
network, allowing for decentralization
and immutability of data. They have a
range of capabilities, including token
creation and management, and they can
be used for a variety of purposes, such
as online marketplaces, social
networks, and more. Despite their many
benefits, developing and deploying a
dApp can be a complex process and
requires a rich understanding of
blockchain technology. That said, there
is great potential in this field so we
are to expect advancements in this area
of blockchain. As more begin to adopt
blockchain, the field of dApps will
continue to evolve and expand with the
world and new use cases and
advancements will be created.

In summary, these are some of the advanced topics in blockchain and smart contract technology that are worth exploring for developers and enthusiasts alike. Understanding these concepts can open up new possibilities for innovation and disruption in various industries. However, it's important to keep in mind that these topics are still in the early stages of development and may not be fully mature yet. As such, they may come with their own set of challenges and risks.

Chapter 7

Conclusion

In conclusion, blockchain smart contracts offer a wide range of potential use cases and opportunities for innovation. From simple token creation and management to complex decentralized applications, smart contracts have the ability to revolutionize traditional industries and business models. However, as with any new technology, there are also risks and challenges that must be addressed. It is important for developers, businesses, and users to be aware of these risks and take the necessary steps to secure and protect their contracts.

The key to successfully implementing smart contracts is to have a thorough understanding of the technology and its capabilities. This includes learning the programming languages used to write smart contracts or working with the right developer that does, interacting with the blockchain network, and monitoring the performance and security of the contracts.

One major area of development in blockchain technology is the increasing use of blockchain in the enterprise sector. Many large companies and organizations are beginning to explore the use of blockchain for supply chain management, digital identity, and other business processes. This is being driven by the increasing recognition of the benefits of blockchain, such as transparency, immutability, and security.

Another important area of development is the continued growth of the decentralized finance (DeFi) ecosystem. DeFi is a set of financial applications built on blockchain technology that aims to provide financial services without the need for intermediaries when doing things like lending, borrowing, and trading. The DeFi ecosystem is still in its early stages, but it has grown rapidly in recent years and is expected to continue to grow in the future.

There is also growing interest in the use of blockchain for social impact and sustainability. Blockchain technology can be used to create more transparent and efficient supply chains for sustainable products, or to track the flow of funds for charitable donations.

The use of smart contracts is also becoming more widespread, and there is a growing interest in the use of smart contract platforms for decentralized autonomous organizations (DAOs), which as previously mentioned, are organizations that are run by code rather than by people. Additionally, new developments in the field of formal verification, which aims to mathematically prove the correctness of smart contracts, are helping to improve the security of smart contracts.

Overall, the future of blockchain and smart contracts is very promising, and it is likely that we will see continued growth and innovation in these areas in the years to come.

In the end, the value of smart contracts lies in the ability to execute complex logic, to automate processes, and to facilitate trustless interactions between parties. As the technology continues to evolve, smart contracts will become even more powerful and will be the backbone of many of the new decentralized applications and ecosystems that will be built on the blockchain.

It is important to note that this is a rapidly evolving field, and there are many new developments and innovations happening all the time. The field of smart contracts is still in its infancy, and it is important to stay informed and up-to-date on the latest trends and best practices.

www.ingramcontent.com/pod-product-compliance
Lightning Source LLC
LaVergne TN
LVHW051608050326
832903LV00033B/4411